Hello, my name is Coco.

About me

My name is _____ .

I am in Year _____ .

Track your progress

As you complete pages in this book, trace over the matching letter here.

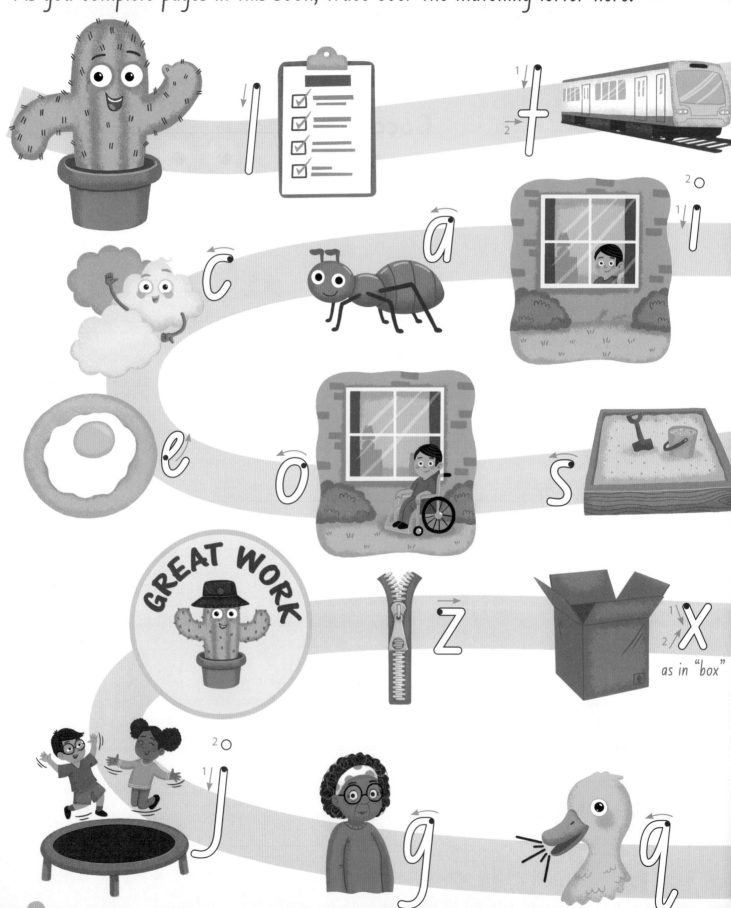

as in "box"

OXFORD UNIVERSITY PRES

Before you begin writing ...

Here are the **3Ps** that will help you with your writing: posture, pencil grip and paper position. You will be reminded about these as you work through the book.

Posture

- Relax your arms.
- Sit back in your chair.
- Make sure your back is straight.

Put your feet flat on the floor.

Pencil grip

How you hold your pencil is important.
- Hold your pencil firmly between your thumb and index finger.
- Balance the pencil on your middle finger.
- Don't grip the pencil too tightly!

Left-handed

Right-handed

Paper position

- Tilt your page.
- Use your non-writing hand to steady the paper.

Left-handed

Right-handed

OXFORD UNIVERSITY PRES

Hand and finger warm-ups

Crocodile snaps (whole arms)

Start with one arm straight above your head and the other extended down one side of your body. Snap your hands together, like a crocodile snapping its jaws. Repeat, with your other arm above your head.

Open, shut them. (hands)

Open, shut them. Open, shut them.
Give a little clap.
Open, shut them. Open, shut them.
Lay them in your lap.
Repeat.

Spider push-ups (fingers)

Place your fingertips together.
Bend and straighten your fingers
while pushing your fingertips
against each other.

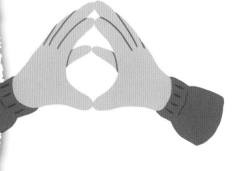

Warm-up patterns for tall letters

Trace the grey lines.

Trace and then copy the numbers.

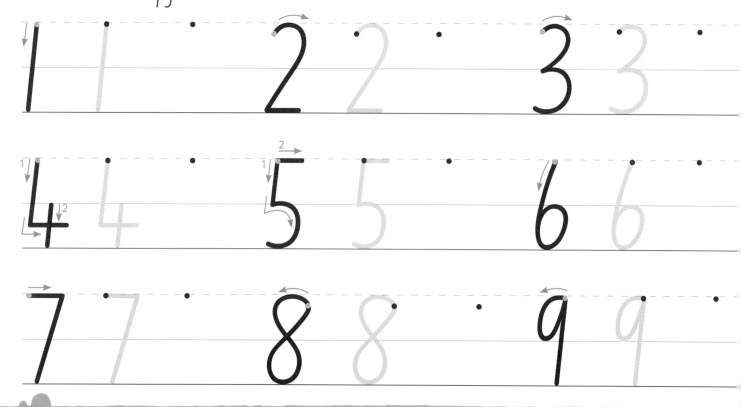

OXFORD UNIVERSITY PRESS

Trace the grey lines.

Trace the numbers.

10   20   30   40

50   60   70

80   90   100

Warm-up patterns for tall letters   7

3Ps Have you checked your posture, pencil grip and paper position?

 Have you done your warm-ups?

above

on

below

Track, trace and copy the letters and words.

list

let lid left list loop

let

L L L L L L L

L

Lee and Lin sit on

Lee

the bench for lunch.

the

Self-assessment

Put a circle around your best letter and word on each page.
Explain your choice to your teacher or classmate.

Tall letter group

3Ps Have you checked your posture, pencil grip and paper position?

 Have you done your warm-ups?

above

on

below

Track, trace and copy the letters and words.

train

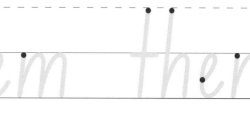 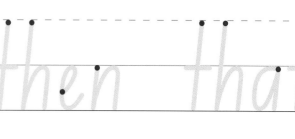

this them then that

this

above
on
below

above
on
below

Tim and Bill went to

Tim

town on the train.

town

Self-assessment

Put a circle around your best letter and word on each page.
Explain your choice to your teacher or classmate.

3Ps Have you checked your posture, pencil grip and paper position?

 Have you done your warm-ups?

above

on

below

f

 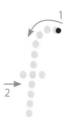 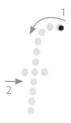

food

Track, trace and copy the letters and words.

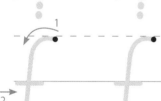

fell   fun   food   from

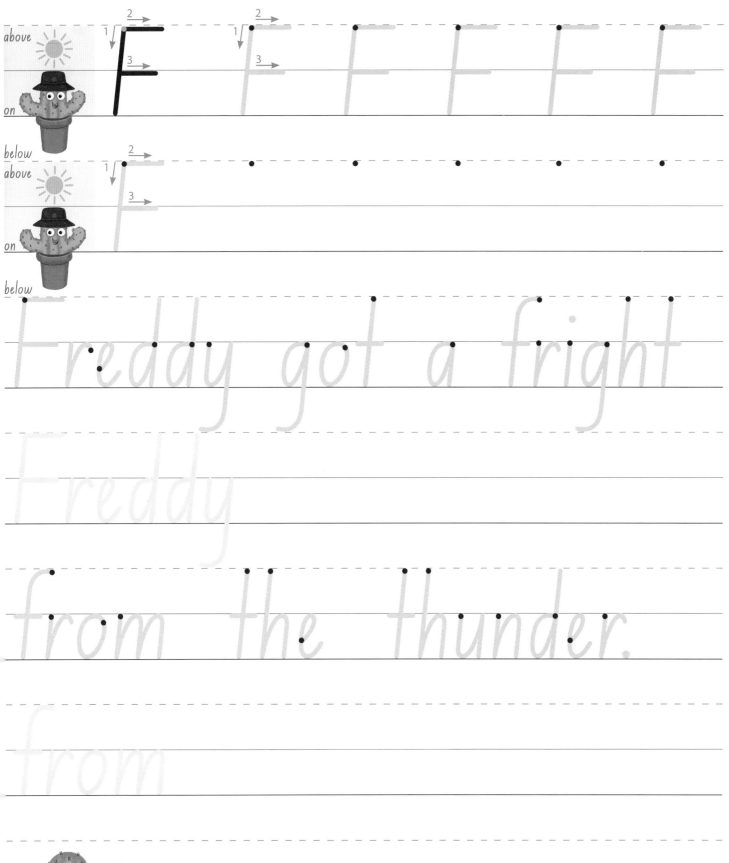

above
on
below

above
on
below

Freddy got a fright

Freddy

from the thunder.

from

3Ps Have you checked your posture, pencil grip and paper position?

 Have you done your warm-ups?

above

on

below

h

Track, trace and copy the letters and words.

h h h h h h h

h h h h h h h

h

had hot his hammer

had

hammer

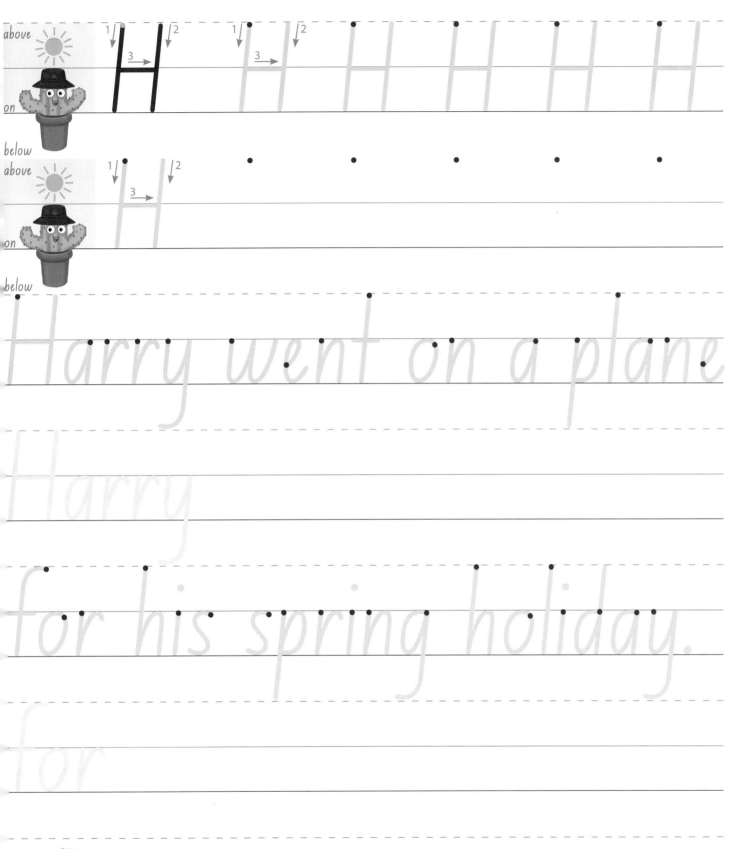

above

on

below

above

on

below

Harry went on a plane

Harry

for his spring holiday.

for

Self-assessment

Put a circle around your best letter and word on each page.
Explain your choice to your teacher or classmate.

3Ps Have you checked your posture, pencil grip and paper position?

 Have you done your warm-ups?

above

on

below

Track, trace and copy the letters and words.

d d d d d d d d

d d d d d d d d

d

did dog doll do dot

did

doll

above
on
below

above
on
below

D D D D D D

D

Dad and Dan played

Dad

with the red dog.

with

Self-assessment

Put a circle around your best letter and word on each page.
Explain your choice to your teacher or classmate.

3Ps Have you checked your posture, pencil grip and paper position?

Have you done your warm-ups?

above
on
below

b

b b b

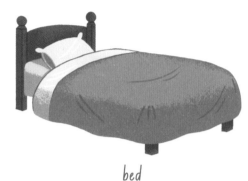

bed

Track, trace and copy the letters and words.

b b b b b b b

b b b b b b b

b

but big bed back

but

above
on
below

above
on
below

B B B B B B B

B

Big and little birds

Big

sing as the sun sets.

sing

Self-assessment

Put a circle around your best letter and word on each page.
Explain your choice to your teacher or classmate.

3Ps Have you checked your posture, pencil grip and paper position?

 Have you done your warm-ups?

above

on

below

k

Track, trace and copy the letters and words.

key

k k k k k k k k k k k k k k

k k k k k k k

k

kit king kittens key

kit

above
on
below

K K K K K K K K

above
on
below

K K K K K K K K

Kip, Kim and Kev

Kip,

kick a ball for fun.

kick

Self-assessment Put a circle around your best letter and word on each page.
Explain your choice to your teacher or classmate.

Tall letter group

Trace the grey lines.

Trace and then copy the numbers.

1 1   ·   2 2   ·   3 3   ·

4 4   ·   5 5   ·   ·   6 6   ·

7 7   ·   8 8   ·   9 9   ·

Trace the grey lines.

Trace the numbers.

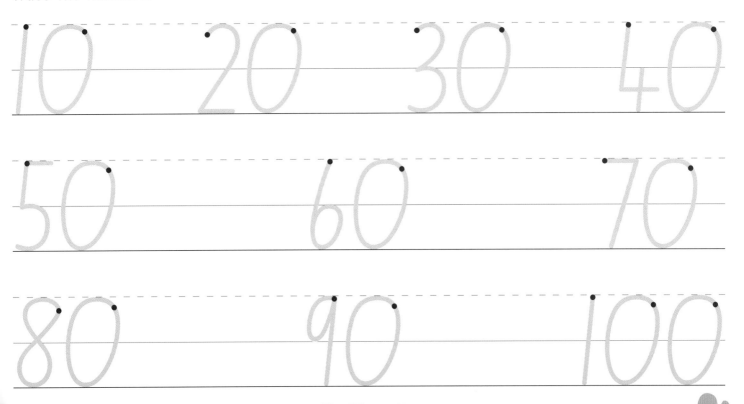

10 20 30 40

50 60 70

80 90 100

OXFORD UNIVERSITY PRESS

3Ps Have you checked your posture, pencil grip and paper position?

 Have you done your warm-ups?

above

on

below

Track, trace and copy the letters and words.

inside

if it in is inside into

if

above

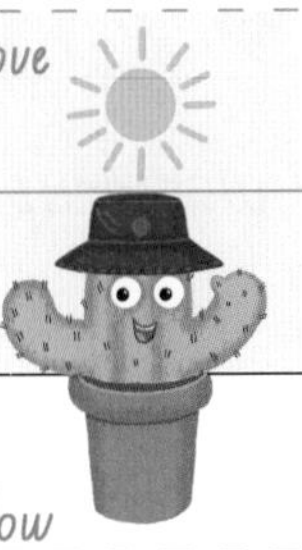

on

below

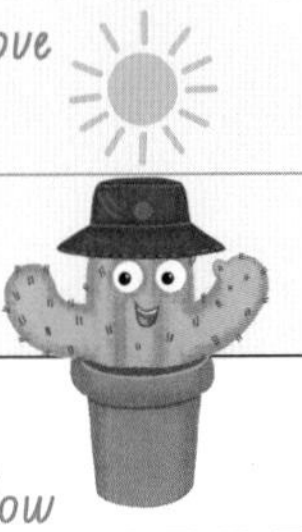

l l l l l l

above

on

below

l

I see a big, bright

I

fish in the pond.

fish

Self-assessment

Put a circle around your best letter and word on each page.
Explain your choice to your teacher or classmate.

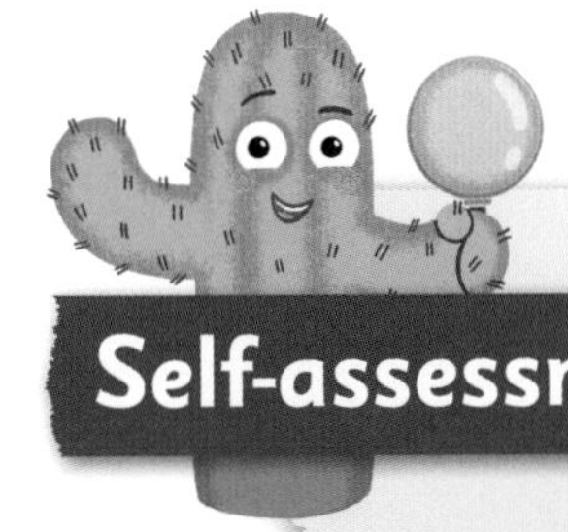

3Ps Have you checked your posture, pencil grip and paper position?

 Have you done your warm-ups?

above
on
below

Track, trace and copy the letters and words.

ant

 a   a   a   a   a   a

 an   am    and    as    ant

an

above

on

below

above

on

below

A A A A A A A

A

Alba raked the grass

Alba

in the back yard.

in

Put a circle around your best letter and word on each page.
Explain your choice to your teacher or classmate.

3Ps Have you checked your posture, pencil grip and paper position?

 Have you done your warm-ups?

above

on

below

Track, trace and copy the letters and words.

c c c c c c c

cloud

---

c c c c c c c

c

can cool cats cloud

can

above

on

below

C C C C C C C C

above

on

below

Cam, the black cat,

Cam,

came back home.

came

Self-assessment

Put a circle around your best letter and word on each page.

Explain your choice to your teacher or classmate.

3Ps Have you checked your posture, pencil grip and paper position?

 Have you done your warm-ups?

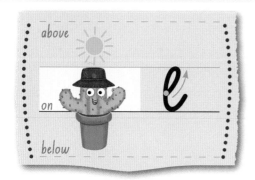

Track, trace and copy the letters and words.

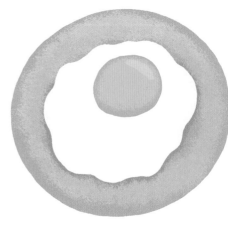

egg

e   e   e   e   e   e   e

e   .   .   .   .   .   .

egg eat each evening

egg

30   Short letter group

OXFORD UNIVERSITY PRESS

above

on

below

above

on

below

Each day for lunch,

Each

Eva eats one egg.

Eva

Self-assessment

Put a circle around your best letter and word on each page.
Explain your choice to your teacher or classmate.

Have you done your warm-ups?

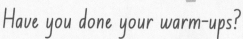

above

on

below

Track, trace and copy the letters and words.

outside

O O O O O O O

o

on off outside odd

on

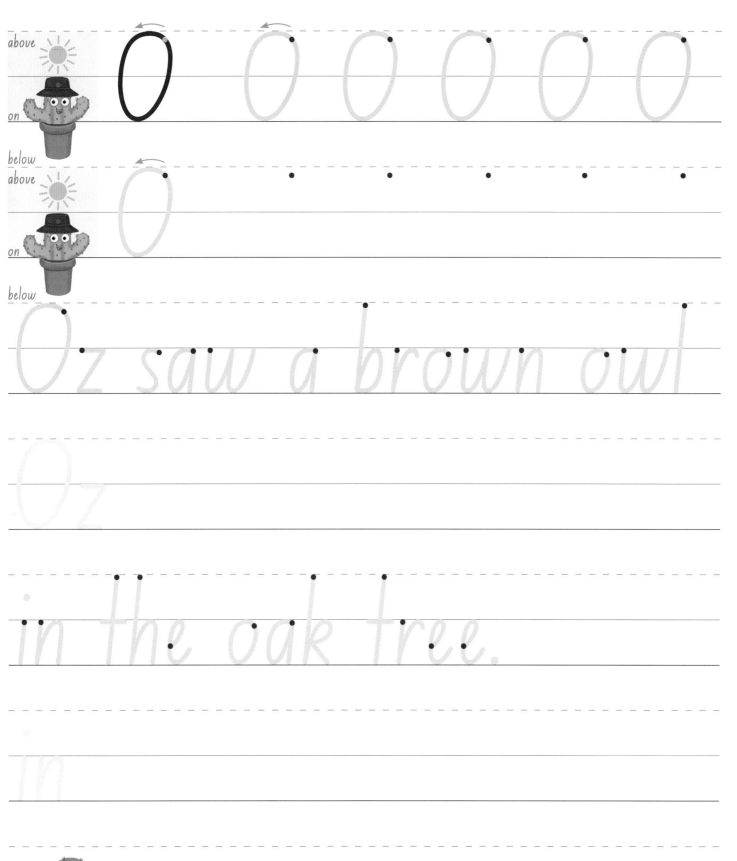

above

on

below

above

on

below

O

Oz saw a brown owl

Oz

in the oak tree.

in

Self-assessment

Put a circle around your best letter and word on each page.
Explain your choice to your teacher or classmate.

3Ps Have you checked your posture, pencil grip and paper position?

 Have you done your warm-ups?

above
on
below

sand

Track, trace and copy the letters and words.

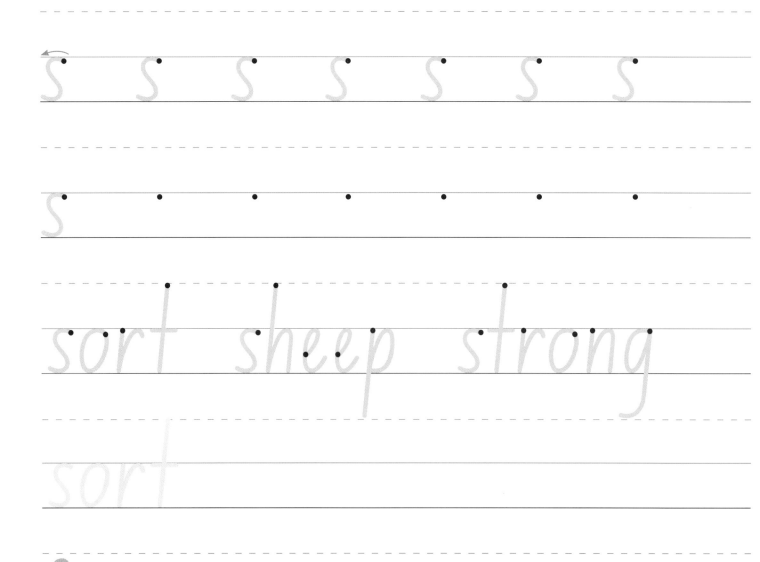

s

s

sort   sheep   strong

sort

OXFORD UNIVERSITY PRESS

above

on

below

above

on

below

S S S S S S

S

Sid and Sam sit on

Sid

the soft, hot sand.

the

Self-assessment Put a circle around your best letter and word on each page.
Explain your choice to your teacher or classmate.

3Ps Have you checked your posture, pencil grip and paper position?

 Have you done your warm-ups?

above

on

below

u

upset

Track, trace and copy the letters and words.

u   u   u   u   u   u   u

u

up   us   upon   upset

up

Short letter group

above

on

below

Uu Uu Uu Uu Uu Uu

above

on

below

Uma felt upset when

Uma

her ice cream fell.

her

Self-assessment Put a circle around your best letter and word on each page.
Explain your choice to your teacher or classmate.

3Ps Have you checked your posture, pencil grip and paper position?

 Have you done your warm-ups?

above

on

below

Track, trace and copy the letters and words.

vet

vet van venue vest

vet

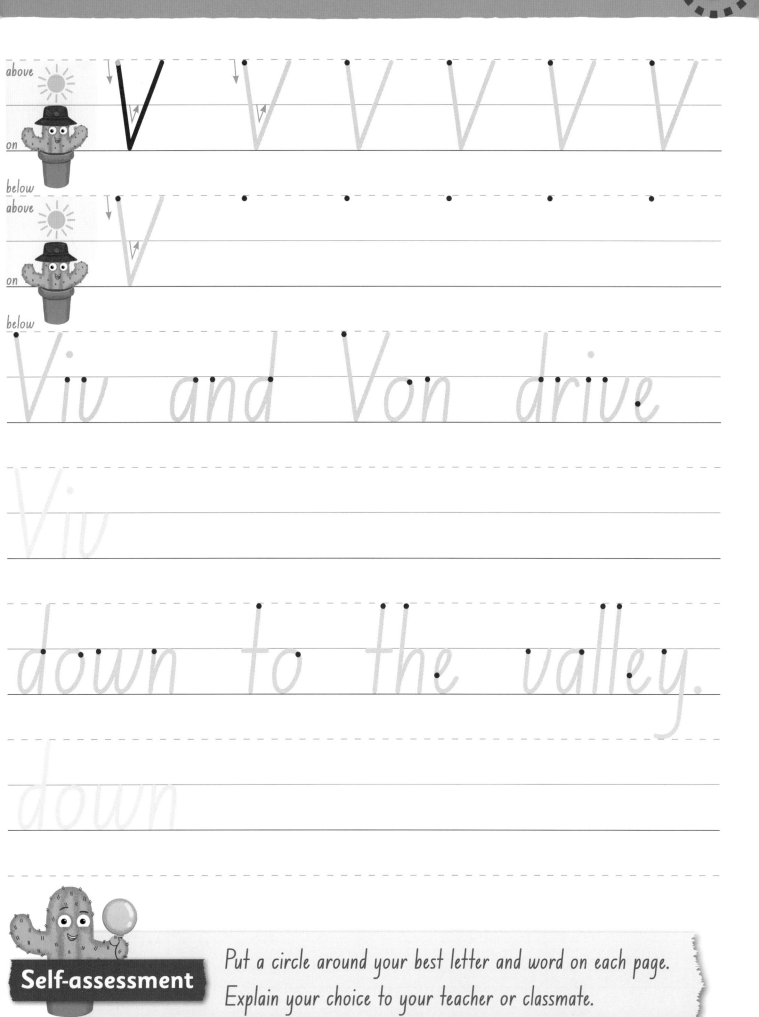

above

on

below

above

on

below

V V V V V V V

V

Viv and Von drive

Viv

down to the valley.

down

Self-assessment   Put a circle around your best letter and word on each page.
Explain your choice to your teacher or classmate.

3Ps Have you checked your posture, pencil grip and paper position?

 Have you done your warm-ups?

above

on

below

Track, trace and copy the letters and words.

wag

w w w w w w w

w

wag wig went way

wag

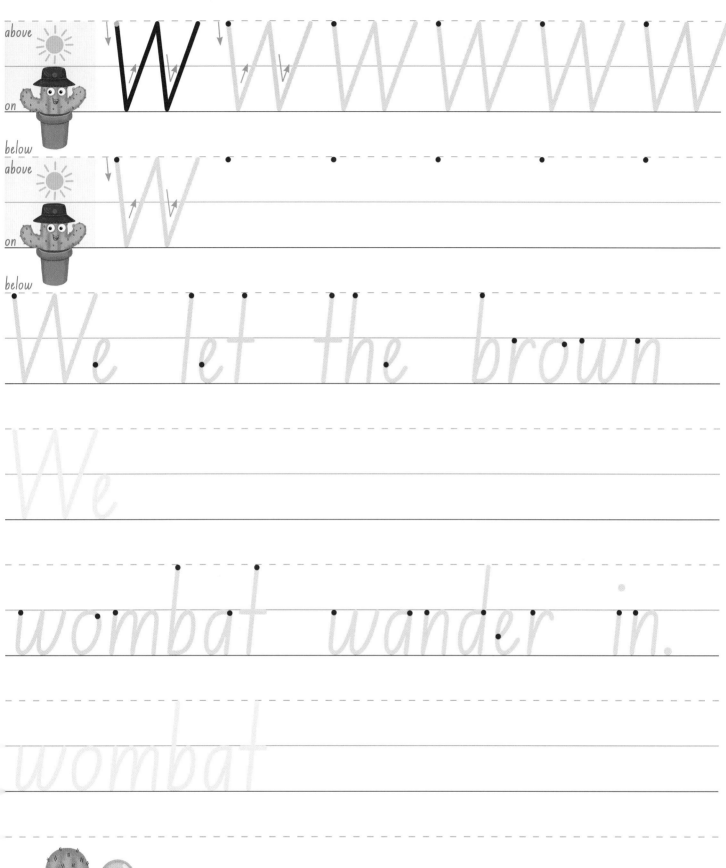

above
on
below

above
on
below

W W W W W W W

W

We let the brown

We

wombat wander in.

wombat

Self-assessment

Put a circle around your best letter and word on each page.
Explain your choice to your teacher or classmate.

3Ps Have you checked your posture, pencil grip and paper position?

 Have you done your warm-ups?

above

on

below

Track, trace and copy the letters and words.

r r r r r r r

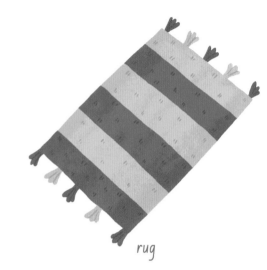

rug

r r r r r r r

r

ran run red read

ran

above

on

below

above

on

below

R R R R R R R

R

Ren put the pet rat

Ren

on the red rug.

on

Self-assessment

Put a circle around your best letter and word on each page.
Explain your choice to your teacher or classmate.

3Ps Have you checked your posture, pencil grip and paper position?

 Have you done your warm-ups?

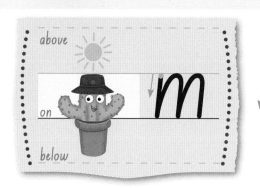
above
on
below

Track, trace and copy the letters and words.

mess

m m m m m m m

m

man moon mess mum

man

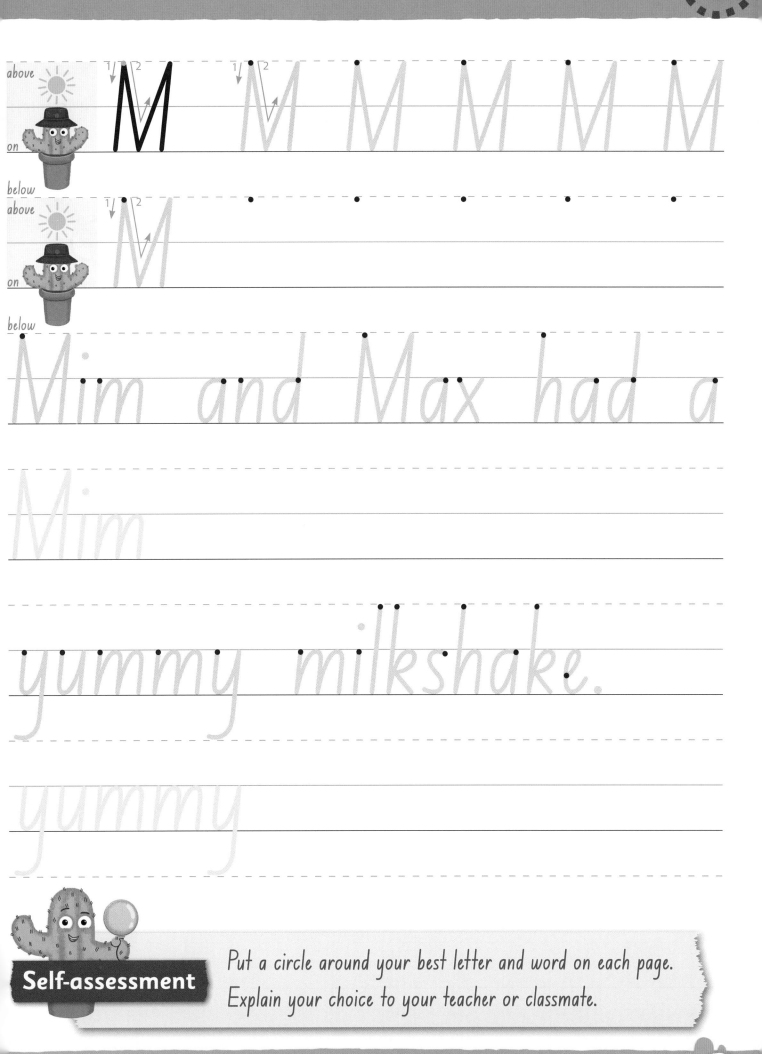

above
on
below

M

above
on
below

M

Mim and Max had a

Mim

yummy milkshake.

yummy

Self-assessment

Put a circle around your best letter and word on each page.
Explain your choice to your teacher or classmate.

3Ps Have you checked your posture, pencil grip and paper position?

Have you done your warm-ups?

above

on

below

Track, trace and copy the letters and words.

note

n n n n n n n

n

not next no note

not

above
on
below

above
on
below

N N N N N N N

Ned and Nell met

Ned

Nimm at the shops.

Nimm

Self-assessment

Put a circle around your best letter and word on each page.
Explain your choice to your teacher or classmate.

3Ps Have you checked your posture, pencil grip and paper position?

 Have you done your warm-ups?

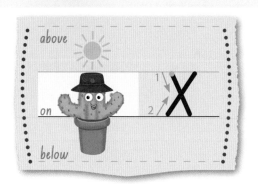

above
on
below

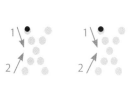

x as in "box"

Track, trace and copy the letters and words.

  X X X X X X X

 x

      box six mix wax text

     box

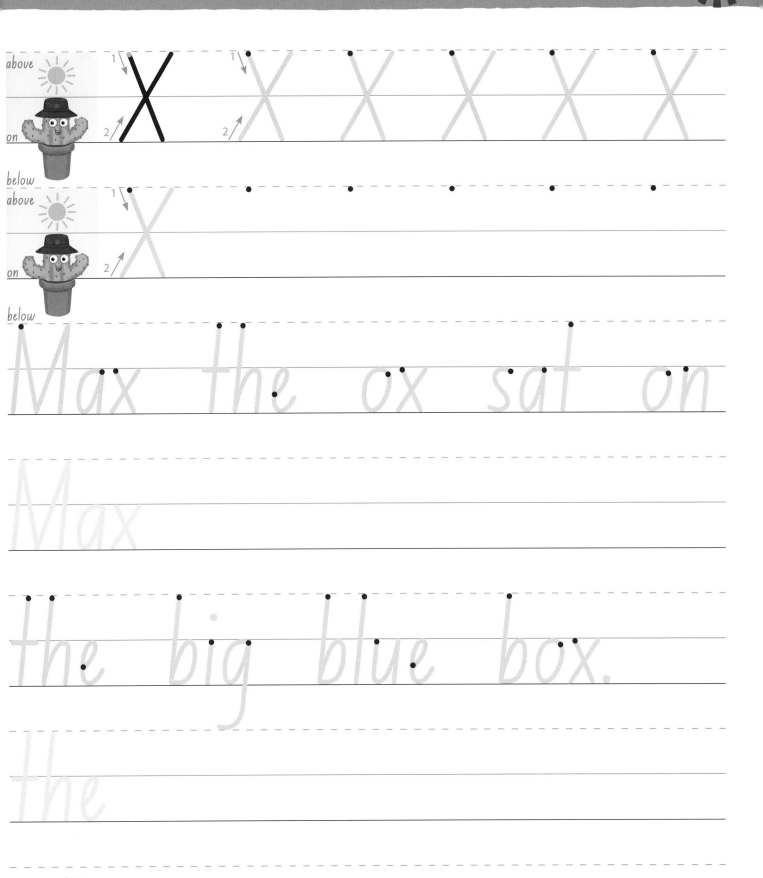

above
on
below

above
on
below

X X X X X X

X

Max the ox sat on

Max

the big blue box.

the

Self-assessment

Put a circle around your best letter and word on each page.
Explain your choice to your teacher or classmate.

3Ps Have you checked your posture, pencil grip and paper position?

 Have you done your warm-ups?

above

on

below

z z z

zip

Track, trace and copy the letters and words.

z z z z z z z

z z z z z z z

z

zig zag zap zip

zig

OXFORD UNIVERSITY PRESS

above

on

below

above

on

below

Zak draws a zigzag

Zak

in the hot sand.

in

Self-assessment

Put a circle around your best letter and word on each page.
Explain your choice to your teacher or classmate.

Warm-up patterns for tail letters

Trace the grey lines.

Trace and then copy the numbers.

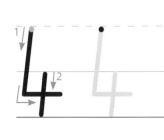 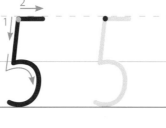 

Trace the grey lines.

Trace the numbers.

10 20 30 40

50 60 70

80 90 100

3Ps Have you checked your posture, pencil grip and paper position?

Have you done your warm-ups?

above

on

below

j

Track, trace and copy the letters and words.

jump

j j j j j j j

j

jog job jets just

jog

above

on

below

above

on

below

J J J J J J

J

Jez and Jo jumped

Jez

over the jam jars.

over

Put a circle around your best letter and word on each page.
Explain your choice to your teacher or classmate.

Tail letter group

3Ps Have you checked your posture, pencil grip and paper position?

 Have you done your warm-ups?

above
on
below

g

Track, trace and copy the letters and words.

grandma

g g g g g g g

g

got going get grandma

got

above

on

below

above

on

below

G G G G G G G

G

Gus the goat lay

Gus

on the green grass.

on

Self-assessment Put a circle around your best letter and word on each page.
Explain your choice to your teacher or classmate.

3Ps Have you checked your posture, pencil grip and paper position?

 Have you done your warm-ups?

above

on

below

Track, trace and copy the letters and words.

quack

q

q

quiz quack quick quit

quiz

above

on

below

above

on

below

Q Q Q Q Q Q Q

Q

Quin the duck quacks

Quin

near the big pond.

near

3Ps Have you checked your posture, pencil grip and paper position?

 Have you done your warm-ups?

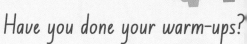

above

on

below

Track, trace and copy the letters and words.

yawn

y y y y y y y

y

yes yap yet yawn

yes

above
on
below

above
on
below

Yin said, "I can't find

Yin

my six yellow yaks."

my

Self-assessment

Put a circle around your best letter and word on each page.
Explain your choice to your teacher or classmate.

OXFORD UNIVERSITY PRESS

Tail letter group   61

Have you done your warm-ups?

above

on

below

p

Track, trace and copy the letters and words.

P P P P P P P

plant

p p p p p p p

p

pink push plant path

pink

above

on

below

above

on

below

P P P P P P

P

Pat went to the pool

Pat

to play and swim.

to

Self-assessment

Put a circle around your best letter and word on each page.
Explain your choice to your teacher or classmate.

Trace the lower- and upper-case letters.

aA   bB   cC   dD

eE   fF   gG   hH

iI   jJ   kK   lL   mM

nN   oO   pP   qQ

rR   sS   tT   uU   vV

wW   xX   yY   zZ

Practise any tricky letters below.